The Polka March

Erik Raichle

To order additional copies of this book, contact:
Xlibris
1-888-795-4274
www.Xlibris.com
Orders@Xlibris.com

Erik Raichle

About the Author
Teacher, farm hand, ranch hand, sheet rocker, greenskeeper, trucker, custom baler, roofer, landscaper, song writer, poet, accordionist, pianist, entertainer, columnist, author, office boy, checkout boy, stock boy, grave digger, trashman, house painter, two family bands, nine children, one wife

1955 Writer for *Miami Daily News*. Inspired by Bill Baggs and Damon Runyon Jr.
1959 University record for the 220 yd dash, at 21 sec (200 meters at 20.8 sec)
1972 – 1990 Polka radio shows over KRFO and KDHL Radio
1989 Minnesota Historical Society's *Teacher of Excellence Award*
1992, 1998 *Who's Who Among America's Teachers*
1993 Steele County Fair harmonica contest winner
2006 *Villages Senior Games* dance contest winner
2008 Flew to Sparta, played accordion for King Leonidas, and washed in the Eurotas River
2012 *Yes There Is A Santa Claus*, a children's book that identifies Santa Claus
2013 *The Greeks Will Save Civilization, Again*, a children's book that will save civilization
2013 *God Is Our Salvation*, a children's book that creates a God for pious people
2014 *The War On Mites*, a children's book that creates a *smart* medical system
2014 *Wake up And Fight For America*, a children's book that solves some world problems

Helen radio	Linda radio	Linda Band	Family Band	Morristown Kids

Polka Music and March Music are brothers

Both have 2/4 Time, or a 1,2 Beat.
In fact, the "skip step" that soldiers use to "get in step",
is the same step that Polka dancers use to dance the Polka.

But, first, I want to tell you a story, a true story.
On Christmas Eve, as we sat in church, listening to the choir, I had a vision.
I saw soldiers marching down the street to Polka music.
Their shiny, black boots were all in step.
As I watched their boots, I began counting their steps: 1,2; 1,2; 1,2; 1,2….

When they took a step with their Right boot, I counted 1.
When they took a step with their Left boot, I counted 2.
I did this for several minutes, and then, **I saw it**.

I saw that when they took a step with their Left boot, the Right boot did not move.
In other words, **It was Zero.**
In other words, the real beat of the Polka March is, **1, 0**.

Immediately, I knew that I had discovered something big, and
I wanted to jump up and shout, *Halleluja*!!
Instead, I whispered to my young son, who was sitting beside me,
"Polka music is the most powerful music in the world."

You see, dear reader, Polka and March music are **Binary**.
And, Binary is the beat of the universe and all modern civilizations.

It's the beat of our heart; the discharge of our brain; the bounce of a ball;
the rotation of the earth around the sun; the ripple of a wave;
the logic in our computer; the oscillator in our radio; the piston in our car, and
the step of 300 Spartans, marching to Thermopylae to save civilization. In fact,
the Greeks created March music to align their new tactical weapon, the phalanx.
And, as they marched, they sang heroic songs, just like soldiers do today.

The Tractor Piston Polka

The Continental Army

My next story happened in 1976.
My students received the Minnesota State School Patrol Award and an
invitation to The Minnesota Safety Council Award Dinner in St. Paul

One of the awards went to a man who dove into the Mississippi River and
saved two women, whose car fell from a bridge, during a storm.
They gave him the

Hero Award

When they asked him why he did it, he replied,
"…it was my family, my church, my school…"
Then, he stopped and said an amazing thing. He said,
"I really don't know why I did it.
"All I remember is a **powerful feeling** to help those women.
"And, *without thinking*, I dove into the river."

Today, we know that powerful feeling was **Heroism.**
Heroism forces us to sacrifice our life to preserve our species.
We cannot control it. It's the most powerful feeling in the world.

When we stand up and give our seat to a handicapped person,
When we step forward for a dangerous mission.
When we mow our neighbor's grass, while they recover from surgery,
When we do anything to help someone, that feeling is Heroism.

Heroes built our civilization. They sacrificed their life to protect us.
Alexander the Great did not conquer the world for fame and fortune.
He conquered the world to bring us civilization.
George Washington and the Continental Army did not fight for money.
They fought to give us freedom.

One of the world's greatest heroes was Joan of Arc, a 17 year old peasant girl,
who loved her country so much, that she went to the king and told him that
God sent her to save his country. At first, the king was doubtful.
Then, Joan whispered a secret in his ear, a secret that only God and the king knew.
Now, the king believed in Joan of Arc and gave her his army.
Like a miracle, she drove the enemy out of her country.

Joan of Arc
January 6, 1412 AD – May 30, 1431 AD

My next story began at the university in Logic class.
The question was,
What is *good*, What is *truth*, and What is *beauty*?
The professor told us that
"beauty is in the eyes of the beholder."
"beauty is a matter of taste."
"there is **no** such thing as Absolute."
In other words, there is no such thing as,
Absolute Good, Absolute Truth, Absolute Beauty

Nine years later,
I taught children in a tiny, Midwestern town, with a population of 700.
Elementary school was on the first floor, high school was on the second, and
graduation was 28 wonderful boys and girls.

On Valentine's Day, they wrote love stories and read them to the class.
To help them with ideas, I wrote on the board things they loved.
They told me they loved
pizza, Big Mac, their dog, football, hunting, fishing, grandma and grandpa…

One year, I don't know what possessed me,
I had them close their eyes, put their head on their desk, and raise their hand
when I read one of the words on the board that they would they die for.
And, every year, they raised their hand for,
God, Family, and Country

At first, I didn't understand.
Then, after seeing the overwhelming number of hands for so many years,
I remembered Logic class and the question,
What is Absolute Good, Absolute Truth, and Absolute Beauty?
And, I saw the answer.
These little children were telling me the answer with their little hands,

God, Family, and Country

After all, if they would die for them, they must be Absolute.

"From the lips of children, we can build a fortress."

God * Family * Country

My last story began as I was walking down the steps of the public library.
At the bottom, a group of businessmen, were standing and talking.
One saw me coming, and said, "Here comes the Polka man."
They all chuckled and added comments.
Everyone in town knew I liked Polka because we had 2 family bands, an
International Polka Queen, a Miss Irish Rose, and a radio show that, for 18 years,
broadcast Polkas all over southern Minnesota and northern Iowa.

But, in 1991, Polka was gone. Schools had **Jazz Bands**, but no **Polka Bands**.
Which is kind of strange, because the people, who settled Minnesota,
were Polka people. The heritage of these merry businessmen was Polka.

Nevertheless, their smugness made me belligerent.
In my heart, I knew I was right, and they were wrong.
So, without thinking, I said,
"What if I told you Polka was the most powerful music in the world?
"What if I told you Polka could change the world?"
"What if I told you…."
That was the day, I began putting all those little stories into a **Big Story**.
I now had Absolute Truth. Those little children showed me.

So, what **are** we going to do about it?

Well,
✓ we're going to write songs about God, family, and country,
✓ we're going to put those songs into Polka March music and
✓ we're going to look for Heroes.
We're going to take our music to
1. religious and military academies,
2. dedication of ships, buildings, monuments,
3. theaters, galleries, sporting events, family events,
4. 4th of July, Veteran's Day, Christmas, New Years, Birthdays, Memorial Day.
Anywhere Heroes go, we go.
Our music will inspire Heroes to
worship God, love their family, and be loyal to our country.
Heroes will reform society and save civilization.

A Medal For Heroes

The Purple Heart

For as long as I can remember, I never liked alcohol.
My grandfather (Pop) didn't like it either. He loved his family, fitness, and horse trading.
His dad died when he was little, so his mother washed clothes for a living.
She also taught him reading and arithmetic at home. She couldn't afford school.

At 18, Pop went to work for the railroad. He worked until noon, then, jumped
the security fence and said, "I can do better than this on my own."

At first, he traded horses; then, cars and trucks; then houses.
When Pop died, his wife collected rent from all the homes he built.

Pop's idol was Bernarr MacFadden, a fitness advocate, who published the magazine,
Physical Culture
Pop read it from cover to cover. It was America's first fitness magazine.

Pop's brother, Owen was a distance runner, who won many races.
One time, Owen made headlines by winning a big race from Altoona to Hollidaysburg.
Interestingly, Owen may be the first person to walk around the world.
We have a picture of him, with worn shoes and dusty pants, at a temple in the Far East.

I got my love for running from Owen, and my love for fitness from Pop.
Neither Pop nor Owen touched alcohol. It was against everything they believed in.

My next story happened as I sat in the high school library, listening to my superintendent
lecture us about student behavior. I reached behind me and pulled a book from the shelf
It was Greek and Roman history.
As I secretly paged thru the book, I came to the Spartans, at the end of the book.
Immediately, I knew who they were. They were Pop, Owen, and me.
They thought, just like us. I liked them so much that I raised my children to be Spartans.
As time went on, I learned that the Spartans saved our civilization.
But, most importantly, the Spartans didn't trust alcohol. They diluted it with water.
As I grew up, I kept losing arguments against alcohol:
"Don't you know that red wine is good for you?"
"Don't you know, the body produces alcohol?"
Then, one day, after losing another argument, it hit me. How does the body treat alcohol?
In 5 minutes, on the Internet, I found that the body treats alcohol as a deadly poison and
sends it directly to the liver to remove the poison. After reading that, I created a slogan,
If the Old Spartans knew what the New Spartans know, they'd prohibit alcohol.

The New Spartans Drink Milk

THE HERO

is the most important person in our life.
God created the Hero to help us, to protect us, and to lead us.

Heroes are all around us.

The man, who dove into the Potomac to save a woman from Flight 90.
The pilot, who landed on the Hudson to save his passengers and crew.
The little boy, who said, "I'll help you, mistah."

All of these people have one thing in their mind, to preserve our species.

In fact,
our greatest scientists, inventors, philosophers, and leaders were heroes.
They worked, day and night, to make a better life for us.
We were always on their mind.

Edison/ electric light	Tesla/ radio	Berners Lee/ internet
McCulloch, Till / stem cells	Newton/ physics	Maxwell/ electromagnet wave
Wright Brothers/ airplane	Benz/ automobile	Travithick/ train
Farnsworth/ TV	Fleming/ penicillin	Hahn/ nuclear energy
Crick, Watson/ DNA	Watt/ steam engine	Babbage/ computer
Guttenberg/ printing press	Bell/ telephone	Goddard, Von Braun/ rockets
Alexander/ Greek Civilization	Joan of Arc/ France	Washington/ America
Martel/ Europe	Evita/ Argentina	Leonidas/ Greece
Socrates/ science	Herodotus/ history	Aristotle/ logic

Heroes are easy to identify because

✓ Heroes are well behaved.
✓ Heroes are respectful.
✓ Heroes are dependable.
✓ Heroes are generous.
✓ Heroes show kindness to all living things.
✓ Heroes always want to do the right thing.
✓ Heroes appear to be a little shy. They are not outspoken.
✓ Heroes are aware of people around them (making sure everyone is OK).
✓ Heroes are usually very intelligent.
✓ Heroes are religious.
✓ Heroes are patriotic.
✓ Heroes love their family.

Heroes are the kind of people we want to be our leader and our neighbor

The Coronation of Miss Irish Rose
Linda Marie Raichle

PARASITES

are the greatest threat to civilization.

Parasites look like us, but they are not. Inside, they says strange things, such as,

"Greed is good." "Never give a sucker a break." "Every one for themself."

Parasites have been around for thousands of years. They are everywhere.
Lawyers, doctors, politicians, executives, even preachers have parasites.

The question is, how did we get these parasites, and how do we get rid of them?
The answer is simple,
We got these parasites because we ignored the Law of Nature that says,
"We want the best."
And, we can get rid of these parasites by following the Law of Nature and say,
"We want the biggest, fastest, strongest, smartest, most attractive,
most talented, most Heroic men and women to be our leaders and our neighbors."
These Heroic men and women will get rid of the parasites.

You're probably wondering, How do we get the best? And, that's simple too:
1. Build a research center that tells us all the things we need to be the best.
2. Build a school to teach these things.
3. Graduate students with documents that prove they are the Best.

These men and women can go anywhere in the world because they will be the best.
People in other countries will want them to be their leaders and their neighbors.
In fact, people in other countries will copy us because it's a good idea.

After we do that, a wonderful thing will happen,
We will control the universe and live forever because these
strong, smart, talented, attractive, Heroic men and women will show us the way.
Then, we will laugh, live, love, and be happy forever.

Then, we will go places, do things, meet people, and enjoy life, forever.
And, all we have to do is,
Get rid of the parasites and keep the best.

Polka has 120 beats per minute, and March has 100 beats per minute.
In other words, a Polka can play a March by slowing down.
And, a March can play a Polka by speeding up.
This is why we can March to a Polka and Polka to a March.
The world's first Polka bands were Marching bands, who loved to play,
The Saints Go Marching In

The Mississippi Music Festival
The world's largest festival

The music begins on the Mississippi and its tributaries and ends in New Orleans

Two weeks of singing, dancing, and more

Keep informed about where and when the bands are playing.

Dutch Hop bands in Denver on the Platte River

Slovenian bands in Pittsburgh on the Ohio River

Polish bands in Chicago on the Chicago River

German bands in New Ulm on the Minnesota River

Country bands in Nashville on the Cumberland River

Western bands in Oklahoma City on the Oklahoma River

Cajun bands in New Orleans on the Mississippi River

Tejano bands in Shreveport on the Red River

Towns that have Polka bands, also, have Marching bands

Razorback Marching Band
Hawkeye Marching Band
Fighting Irish Marching Band
Redcoat Marching Band
Million Dollar Marching Band
Spartan Marching Band
Mountaineer Marching Band
Cornhuskers Marching Band

Aggie Marching Band
All American Marching Band
Minute Man Marching Band
Longhorn Marching Band
Royal Dukes Marching Band
Bruin Marching Band
Trojan Marching Band
Pride of the Southland Marching Band

Polka bands, Marching bands, and more will be at the Festival.

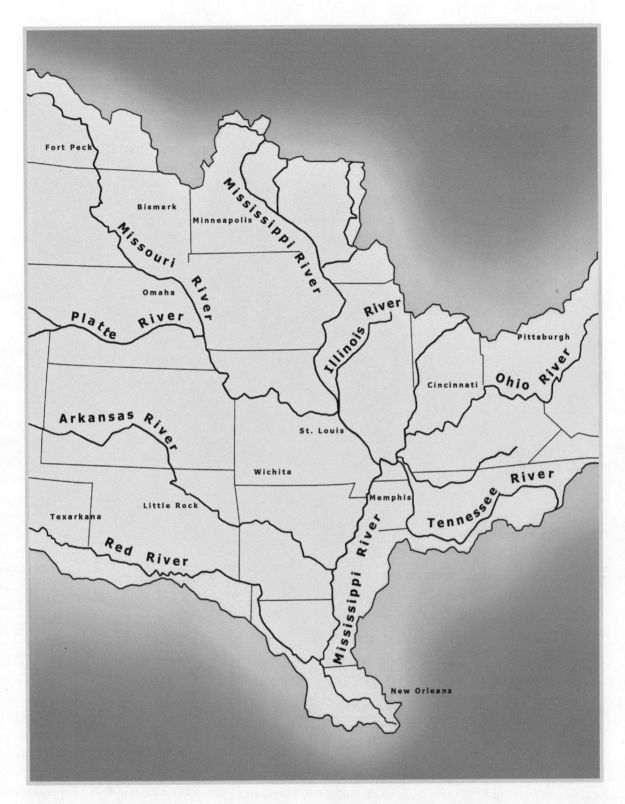

Some of the rivers in the Mississippi Music Festival

The Mississippi Music Festival

Here are some of the cities, bands, and people you will see at the Festival.

Mississippi River

Minneapolis	St. Paul	Memphis	New Orleans
Baton Rouge	St. Cloud	La Crosse	Dubuque
Natchez	Chester	Rock Island	Davenport
Burlington	Wittenberg	Vicksburg	Red Wing
Brainerd	Arabi	St. Louis	Cairo

Ohio River

Pittsburgh	Cincinnati	Louisville	Evansville
Steubenville	Owensboro	Wheeling	Portsmouth
Paducah	Parkersburg	Ashland	Cairo

Platte River

Denver	Walden	Littleton	Greeley
Casper	Scotts Bluff	Fort Laramie	Grand Island

Arkansas River

Pueblo	Fort Smith	Little Rock	Salida
Tulsa	Wichita	Garden City	Dodge City

Red River of the South

Shreveport	Bossier	Wichita Falls	Dennison
Fulton	Elmer	Fulton	Texarkana

Swedish Schottische Band	Polish Polka Bands	Scottish Bagpipe Bands
Dutch Hop Bands	Irish Celli Bands	Viennese Quartet Bands
Slovenian Polka Bands	German Oompa Bands	Swiss Yodeling Bands
Latvian Marching Bands	Symphony Polka Bands	Cossack Bands
Croatian Bands	Ukrainian Hopak Bands	Norwegian Bands
Russian Bands	Latvian Polka Bands	Irish Bagpipe Bands
Finlander Bands	Rumanian Bands	Czech Polka Bands
Portuguese Fado	Hungarian Czardas Bands	Italian Calabrese Bands
French Chanson	Spanish Flamenco Bands	Greek Bousouki Bands
Brazilian Fandango	Colombian Vallenato	Argentine Tango Bands
French Hurdy Gurdy	Lithuanian Bands	Estonian Tuulikki Bands
Magyar Bands	Tejano Polka Bands	Conjunto Polka Bands

The Polka Salute

Work and Pray

for

God, Family, and Country

The Morristown Kids
World's First And Only Elementary School Polka Band

KRFO Polka Radio Show: 1972 - 1991
Dad, Teresa, Brian, Kurt

Raichle Family Polka Band 1972 - 1982

Little Linda Polka Band 1983 - 1991

Polka Dancers
Kurt and Teresa Raichle

Hearts that hear the Polka beat smile.
Hands that hold their children's hands smile.
But, if we lose the Polka beat,
Saddness falls on little feet.
Who will hold those tiny hands, now?
But, if we lose the Polka beat,
Saddness falls on little feet.
Who will hold those tiny hands, now?

Where have all the Polka bands gone?
We could sing and dance until dawn.
Now, the nights are long and sad,
Nothing left of dreams we had.
Where have all the Polka bands gone?
Now, the nights are long and sad,
Nothing left of dreams we had.
Where have all the Polka bands gone?

All around the sound of decay.
People living just for today.
Will the darkness ever end?
Will our music live again?
Lord have mercy on us, we pray.
Will the darkness ever end?
Will our music live again?
Lord have mercy on us, we pray

Then, a voice spoke into the night,
Sharper then the blade of a knife.
"Oh, my children, do not fear.
"Say these words for all to hear,
'God, family, country gives us life.'
"Oh, my children, do not fear.
"Say these words for all to hear,
'God, family, country gives us life.'

"Go to all the nations, rejoice.
"Tell the people they have a choice.
"Keep the happy Polka beat.
"Teach it to your children's feet.
"Let them hear the joy in your voice.
"Keep the happy Polka beat.
"Teach it to your children's feet.
"Let them hear the joy in your voice."

CPSIA information can be obtained
at www.ICGtesting.com
Printed in the USA
BVHW020833080719
552846BV00005B/83/P